21
f
26
mp
31
35
pp
mp
40
f rit.

Mom's Pick-up Truck

Giocoso ♩= 144-168

Original music and lyrics
by Al Rita

16
back she'll chuck. That's why Mom loves her pick - up truck. When shop-ping at the
p
20
mall, my moth-er has a ball. 'Cause she knows she can haul
25
an - y - thing at all. (Beep beep, beep beep, beep beep, beep beep.) When
f
mf
29
I grow up, with an - y luck, I'm goin' to drive a pick - up truck. For
33
now I'll ride with my friend, Chuck, in - side my moth - er's pick - up truck.
(Beep beep!)
f

In the Hall of the Mountain King

Edvard Grieg
Arr. by Wesley Schaum

Misterioso 𝅗𝅥 = 120-140

*PEER GYNT STORY. Peer Gynt is a young man who has many fantastic adventures in Norway. In one episode, he visits the king of the trolls, an ugly dwarf who lives in an enchanted cave beneath a mountain. The king has grotesque features with big ears and a black beard.

17
mf
21
f
25
sfz
sfz
29
ff

Alien Yard Sale

Original music and lyrics by
Larry Rapshaw

Allegro ♩= 104-116

17
We have an at - om shuf - fler, doo dee doo. We have a space ship muf - fler, doo dee doo.
21
All sorts of vir - tu - al hand - y - man's dreams, Moon boots, zoot suits, ev - 'ry - thing, it seems.
25
Vor - tex trav - el bags, hov - er - craft cars, bug - gy eye shades that glow like the stars.
29
D.C. al fine
Four - fin - ger gloves and tel - e - path - ic beams. Come, buy it all, or just come, by all means.

William Tell March

Gioachino Rossini
Arr. by Wesley Schaum

Vivace ♩= 168-192